CAREERS IN THEATRE, MUSIC, AND DANCE

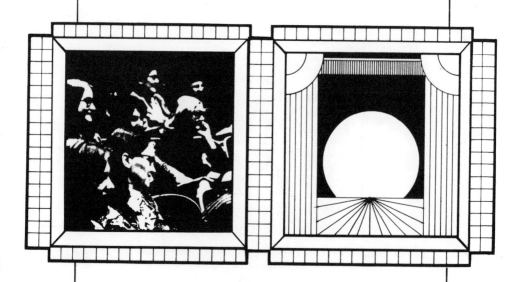

BY LOUISE HORTON

ILLUSTRATED BY NEIL STUART

A Career
Concise Guide

FRANKLIN WATTS

NEW YORK | LONDON | 1976

CAREERS IN
THEATRE,
MUSIC,
AND DANCE

To the memory of my mother,
who gave me my love for the performing arts

Library of Congress Cataloging in Publication Data

Horton, Louise
    Careers in theatre, music, and dance.

    (A Career concise guide)
    Bibliography: p.
    Includes index.
    SUMMARY: Describes careers in theater,
dance, and music, including those behind the
scenes. Discusses the training needed for such jobs
and lists some outstanding schools in each area.
    1. Performing arts—Vocational guidance—
United States—Juvenile literature. [1. Performing arts
—Vocational guidance. 2. Vocational guidance]
I. Stuart, Neil.   II. Title.
PN1580.H6   790.2'023   76–20513
ISBN 0–531–01205–0

The Author Thanks

Mary L. T. Brown
John Gambling, WOR, New York
Mary Greene, casting director
Mary Alan Hokanson
Celeste Holm
Violet Lane
Philip Nolan, director, The New York Academy of Theatrical Arts
Mary Margaret Regan
Carlotta Reiner
Betty J. Stillman

A very special thanks to The Juilliard School, New York:
Dr. Peter Mennin, President
Saul Goodman, head, Percussionist Faculty
Martha Hill, director, Dance Division,
and a most cooperative staff

and to

Earle Goodwin, B.M., B.A., M.S.M., Oberlin College,
Union Theological Seminary,
Organist for First Church of Religious Science,
broadcasting weekly coast to coast from
Alice Tully Hall, Lincoln Center, New York

CONTENTS

CAREERS IN THEATRE, MUSIC, AND DANCE

THE
CHALLENGE
OF THE
PERFORMING
ARTS

When Christopher Marlowe in 1587 walked into The Theatre in London (so called because when it was originally built it was the only building in London deliberately designed to be used as a theatre), he did something he wasn't supposed to do in the performing arts—he challenged tradition. And young artists have been challenging tradition ever since.

In 1587 London audiences were used to seeing productions like *Gorboduc* and *The Spanish Tragedy,* plays with wooden characters and long-winded, stilted, monotonous verse. But this was the way plays were supposed to be written, and everyone wrote them that way.

Until Marlowe. He strode into the theatre, slapped a manuscript down on the director's table, and said, "No! *This* is the way to write a play." His play, *Tamburlaine the Great,* fresh, new, dramatically exciting with its "mighty line," was an overnight hit. Young Marlowe, at twenty-three, had changed the whole direction of theatrical history.

In 1899 a young dancer performed at a New York charity affair. She astonished and shocked many in her audience by appearing barefoot and scantily clad, and relying only on the natural motions of her body for her dance movements. The audience, used to classical ballet only, found the girl's performance upsetting.

One newspaper reporter described her movements as "painful" and deplored the fact that she planned to introduce her dancing to English society: "She has fully determined on this reckless course," he wrote, "which is sad, considering we are at peace with England at present."

No one now recalls the name of this sarcastic critic. But everyone knows the name of Isadora Duncan, innovator of modern dance and one of the great performing artists of our century.

It is the challenge of artists like these that you have inherited. But make no mistake. If you choose a career in one of the performing arts, you "marry" it, for better or for worse. Few other careers are as demanding. And it takes at least a spark of genius to get to the big time—to Broadway, to the Metropolitan Opera, to the New York City Ballet, to Hollywood, or to NBC. But if you are really "smitten," you won't care. You will love all of it, the agony and the ecstasy.

The technological revolution has given the performing arts new ways to reach audiences, bringing theatre, ballet, opera, and symphony to many who had never seen them before. But it has changed little in the fundamental techniques of the actor, dancer, singer, or musician. For this reason it is not wise at the outset to aim at a career in television, radio, or film, so these disciplines are touched on only briefly in this book.* Spend your time now mastering the essential techniques of your chosen profession, whether it be dancer, singer, actor, or director. All the information you will need for that *is* in the following pages.

You should think now also about your uniqueness and about how you can someday bring that uniqueness to others. Perhaps a potential Marlowe or Duncan is reading this book right now. Perhaps it is you. Come explore the world of the theatre, music, and dance and find out.

* For details, see the Career Concise Guide *TV and Radio Careers,* by D. X. Fenten, also published by Franklin Watts.

THEATRE

THE ACTOR

New York! Does the city and its golden street, Broadway, beckon you? Perhaps you already see yourself in the spotlight at the Helen Hayes Theatre, bowing to the applause of a first-night audience. The next day *The New York Times* hails you as Broadway's "shining new star."

Wake up! Before anything like that dream can come true, you must face the realities of a career in the professional theatre.

What Is Acting?

Acting is playing a part. It is impersonating a character other than yourself in the theatre, in the movies, or on radio or television. But it is not as easy as it appears. You will need more than the talent the home folks admired when you decide to tackle Broadway.

Talent is necessary, but a good education can start you on your way by giving you thorough training in the art of acting and in disciplining your body, voice, mind, and imagination.

Then you will need experience—you must learn to act by acting. You must acquire technical skill and then allow experience to develop it into artistry. It is this that gives a star the personal aura that comes across in his or her every expression, movement, and voice inflection.

You may not always achieve the desired effect on stage at first. Don't be stopped by this, but don't ignore it either. As successful comedienne Phyllis Diller said, "When you do something to get a laugh, you have to get it or you're a failure." In other words, you must always evaluate yourself and your performance realistically if you want to be a success.

Training/Education

Should you go to a specialized school or to college to study acting?

The first usually puts most of its emphasis on acting itself. The second stresses the art but gives the student a wider background. Many college and university theatres are headed by professionally experienced directors, and students are trained in all aspects of the theatre.

The usual university group puts on its own productions. Faculty members and students act in and stage these plays themselves. Another type will invite a well-known performer or director to head the school's acting company for a semester, to give students a chance to study under some of the best talent in the business.

A third type maintains its own resident company of professional actors and directors. Students may be limited to bit parts, walk-ons, and crowd scenes. Even so, contact with professionals does often prove beneficial.

If you are thinking of studying at one of the specialized New York acting schools, send for school catalogs now and study them carefully before applying. Learn which schools demand pre-training (the Juilliard School, for example) and which do not (the New York Academy of Theatrical Arts is one). An audition and interview are almost always required.

Philip Nolan, director of the New York Academy, said that each beginning student is automatically put on four weeks' probation. At the end of the month a decision is made as to whether or not the student will be allowed to continue.

Nolan explained the standards on which this decision is based: attendance and punctuality, honest performance, responsiveness to direction, and acting ability. Any good theatre school will expect the same from its students.

In acting class you will learn how to determine the relationship between your part and the whole play, how to memorize with ease, how to enter, exit, and cross a stage effectively, how to project the character you are portraying, and how to work with the director, the other actors, and the backstage crew.

You will learn how to relax and how to concentrate. You will study characterization and the use of your imagination and of your sense and emotional memories. You will experiment with period as well as modern roles, with improvisation, and with comedy and tragedy.

Your acting tools are your body and your voice. Dance and

[7]

pantomime are fine disciplines for the body. For the voice you must develop clarity, resonance, variety of pitch and inflection, and projection, and eliminate any regional accent in favor of "stage diction."

The stage demands projection of voice and gestures to carry across the footlights. On film, because the camera exaggerates, the actor must underplay instead. In television, acting is for the small TV screen and is done almost entirely with the face. On radio, it is your voice that does all the work.

Sooner or later you will meet the Stanislavski method of acting, commonly known as "the method," which trains you to act as though an imaginary situation were real, to create the illusion of "the first time." If you are successful, your acting will appear unrehearsed.

While in school you should also learn a skill such as typing or stenography. You can't break into theatre right away, so it's a good idea to have some other way to pay the rent.

Finally, if there is a children's theatre, a high school drama group, or a community playhouse in your town, by all means get involved!

Opportunities

Taking your first steps toward Broadway is important. Fortunately, if you live in certain areas, you may be able to reach Broadway by following this two-step plan:

(1) Local theatres: These may be seasonal, like the Eugene O'Neill Memorial Theatre in Waterford, Connecticut, or year-round, like the Hedgerow Theatre in Moylan, Pennsylvania, or your university theatre. Once you get in, you must study, practice, and rehearse on your own, with the purpose of improving and polishing your acting technique.

Why? Because your aim is to be the *best* in your local playhouse. It may not be easy, but it's necessary so that you will be noticed by scouts from the

(2) Regional theatres: These theatres, scattered around the country, keep in touch with Broadway through the Theatre Communications Group, 355 Lexington Ave., New York City.

Theatres like the Alley Theatre in Houston and the Arena Stage in Washington, D.C., are the closest thing we have to repertory. Because they all have strong directors, they offer valuable experience to the young performer.

Once you are cast in a regional theatre production, you have a new aim—to become the *best* in that group. If you do, you can practically be sure of getting onto Broadway itself.

When you finally reach the magic street, don't despise small parts at first; at least you may be noticed. However, one actress cautions beginners *not* to try to stand out in crowd scenes. "Turn aside," she said. "If you become identified with too many crowd scenes, it may ruin your chances for something better." This also applies to film.

While you are trying out for a part, try to ignore the impersonal manner of those holding the auditions. These people are seriously looking for the right person for each role. Keeping this in mind should make it easier for you to look, act, and speak with confidence.

Actress Violet Lane advises that you should always arrive early for auditions so that you can relax and look over the script. "Don't be afraid to speak up and ask the director what he or she is looking for in the part. Don't rush. When your turn comes, walk out on stage with the script in your hand and read from it. Don't try to prove yourself an instant study."

If you are asked back, study both your part *and* the whole play, if possible. And choose carefully what you wear. If you are trying out for the part of a maid, for example, don't show up in your most sophisticated ensemble. The director may have difficulty imagining you in the part.

If you get the role, memorize it immediately. Only after you learn your part thoroughly can you cooperate with the director.

There will be an average of three weeks' rehearsal (a week or less for summer stock) plus a road tour or some previews before opening night.

Actors' Equity
Your first acting job with regional theatre will make you eligible

to join Actors' Equity Association, a union formed to protect actors' rights.

When you actually land a contract with a Broadway producer, you *must* join Actors' Equity if you are not already a member. Equity sets salary minimums. The Broadway minimum is $265 a week, on tour $375 a week. Extras, sometimes called "background people," can earn $58.50 a day working in television, but not nearly as much working in the theatre. If you get a walk-on part and also understudy one of the important roles, you get the minimum, $265. How much above the minimum you make obviously depends on your reputation as well as on the bargaining ability of your agent.

There are many other advantages to joining Equity. All the shows being cast on Broadway, with a description of the roles available, are listed at the Equity office, and you can stop there and check them out each day. These audition notices can be used by Equity members only. "Open calls," which can be used by nonmembers as well, are posted only for off-Broadway and off-off-Broadway productions.

The Equity Library Theatre. Partly sponsored by Equity, this theatre, at 103rd Street and Riverside Drive, New York City, serves as a showcase of young theatre talent. The season runs from October to May, with one play every five weeks or so. The theatre plays to invited audiences of important directors and producers.

How do you know if you should take the plunge and come to New York? When I put this question to actress Celeste Holm, she quickly responded, "Your reason for wanting to act must be bigger than yourself." She pointed out that there are basically two kinds of people who aspire to the theatre: those who want to show off, and "those who want the more important experience of bringing something to life on the stage, a special something that the people out there in the audience might not pay attention to if they were not reminded of it by the actor's art."

If you understand—and *feel*—what Miss Holm is saying, you

probably should come to New York. But if you don't, then reconsider.

THE PLAYWRIGHT

When you hear the word *theatre,* what do you see in your mind's eye? A stage with a setting, and actors moving about in attractive costumes? Do you perhaps give a brief thought to the director who staged it all?

How about the playwright? Without that weaver of dreams and realities, there would be nothing for the director to stage or the actors to perform.

A playwright is, obviously, a writer of plays. But the art of playwriting actually involves the mastering of two arts—the art of writing itself and the specialized art of dramaturgy.

Before you attempt a play, you must be able to write well. The craft of writing is a complete discipline in itself. Then you must learn the additional skills needed to write for the theatre.

Dramaturgy refers to the art of writing for the theatre. But for you as playwright, achieving success in that art is not easy. It means that your written dialogue must come to life on stage and form for the audience a unified and moving experience.

It also means you must fully understand all the facets of stage direction and production, and use that knowledge in creating your play. Only then will your work deserve serious consideration by a theatrical producer. Reading this book's entire section on theatre careers can introduce you to the various aspects you need to know.

Of all writing careers except poetry, playwriting is probably the hardest in which to "make it big." Play*wright* is spelled that way for a very good reason. A *wright* is a person who constructs something. And that is exactly what writers of plays do —build or construct their plays brick on dramatic brick.

Approaches to writing plays differ widely. Some dramatists change their plot outline several times, then write and rewrite laboriously. Others think their plays through first, then write swiftly, often completing them in a few weeks. But success in writing plays can be achieved only by experience. You must write, write, write.

Training/Education

A college education offers you two principal advantages: (1) a broad background in the history and practice of the theatre and in the works of the great dramatists; and (2) well-planned assignments to help you master the fundamentals of playwriting. And you might even see your own play staged.

The training you get in college will enable you to learn in depth what playwriting is all about. John Gassner, in his classic text *Producing the Play,* writes: "The drama presents *a sequence of situations* in which characters express themselves *through what happens to them, what they do or* (even) *fail to do."* (The emphasis is Gassner's.) This basic statement can be used to describe *all* types of theatre. You will study the classics as well as modern plays, but always beware of merely imitating them. Be yourself.

The three most essential techniques to master are plot structure, characterization, and dialogue.

In most three-act plays the first act presents the problem, the second leads up to a crisis, and the last act resolves the crisis. In fact, most plays, even one-act plays, use this same three-part dramatic development, or plot structure.

Furthermore, each act is broken down into many tiny scenes. To the director a new scene begins with each actor's entrance, exit, or re-entrance. For example, in Act 1, Scene 2 of Sheridan's *The Rivals,* there are eleven or twelve such "mini" scenes, although the audience sees all of them as one complete unit.

As you plot your play, you must build into it both conflict and suspense. It must hold the attention of the audience. Characterization is important here, because you must tell the theme of your play in terms of people. The audience must believe in your characters and care about what happens to them.

You create your characters mainly through your dialogue, so have someone read it aloud to you and listen carefully. If it *sounds* right, it probably *is* right. A special problem for the writer of radio drama is to indicate time, place, and setting, as well as character, through dialogue.

Your play, whether for stage, screen, radio, or TV, and no matter what period it is set in, must speak to today's audiences. If it speaks truly, it will speak for all time.

Opportunities

Opportunities abound for the young playwright who knows where to look. Cost alone makes a beginner's work too risky for Broadway, so head with your material to the many off-Broadway and off-off-Broadway theatres instead. Even though much of the material produced here is experimental, a truly good drama may become a hit and later move on to Broadway. Revenues from off-Broadway may be small (low royalties, meager box-office receipts), but getting your play produced in an off-Broadway theatre does offer invaluable experience.

First, however, try your university, community, or children's theatre, to get the reaction of real audiences. There are hundreds of these theatres around the country, and all are hungry for good dramas, comedies, and musicals. And they do pay thousands of dollars in royalties each year.

Your chances of having your play produced increase if you make the action clear-cut, and keep the number of set changes minimal, and the cast small.

Children's theatre offers a first-rate opportunity for the student interested in learning how to write a play. You can't fool children. They will laugh your play off the stage if any part of it is phony. But if you can hold their attention through three whole acts and keep them asking what's going to happen next, you can be sure you have learned a lot.

Is an agent important? On Broadway, yes. But that agent must have something really good to offer a producer, a "sure thing, a hit." And you must turn out this "sure thing" if you expect an agent to take you on. Whether or not the agent should charge a fee for reading your manuscript is highly debatable. Those who do charge justify it on the grounds of time, expense, and the need to cut down on undesirable manuscripts. But many respectable agents do not charge.

If a New York producer considers a play for production, the author is paid a small option, perhaps $500. This means that the producer has exclusive rights to the play for about three months. It is *not* a guarantee that the play will be produced. At the end of three months the option may be renewed with a second payment to the author. Even if the play is finally accepted, it may be a year before it actually reaches the rehearsal stage.

Once you are paid an option, you are eligible to join the Dramatists Guild, whose purpose is to protect and promote the professional interests of its members. It also acts with the Authors Guild on matters of joint concern to authors and playwrights, such as copyright protection and freedom of expression.

When your play does reach rehearsal, remember that the director and the actors want your play to be a hit as much as you do. So listen to and try to learn from any criticism.

If your ultimate aim is Broadway, where the big money is, then regard each effort you make as a stepping-stone in that direction. Authors of Broadway hits make thousands of dollars and often make additional thousands from subsidiary rights— road shows, Hollywood, television, performances abroad, even amateur performances that pay royalties year after year.

But there are precious few hits per season on Broadway. So beware: if you aim too high, you may get nowhere.

A word of encouragement from author Jean Dalrymple: "The [truly competent] playwright today has the best chance of financial return, because good material is so scarce that a produced work, especially if it has some humor in it, is eagerly bid for by the television and film companies."

So spin some dreams and make them come alive for you and for theatre audiences everywhere.

THE PRODUCER

A producer's main function is to obtain the money to launch a show and keep it afloat until it can pay for itself. This cannot happen until all initial expenses are paid. But a producer can make it big on Broadway if everything clicks. People like Cheryl Crawford, David Merrick, Gilbert Miller, Harold Prince, and Richard Rodgers have made themselves a name in this field.

What qualities must a producer have? First, a business head for the theatre's peculiar financial needs. Second, a reputation for stability and wisdom that will encourage "angels" to lay their money on the line. And third, the ability to spot a potential hit.

A producer usually backs a production because an exciting play script has turned up. The producer must then select a director to bring that script to life. When you see in a show's program "produced and directed by ———," listing one name, it means that the producer has directed his or her own show.

After a bond is placed with Equity, usually to cover salaries for the entire cast for two weeks, and a playhouse is found, the show can be considered well on its way.

Training/Education/Opportunities

What background is necessary? Knowledge of all phases of theatre, of theatre management, and of business techniques. Experience as actor and director can be helpful.

Opportunities? They are everywhere—*as long as you have or can get the money.*

THE DIRECTOR

A director is someone who puts together all aspects of a theatrical production to create a single dramatic effect. Joshua Logan believes that every good director needs "a good eye for pictorial composition and movement, an ear for dialogue and diction, a charm that keeps a big company working happily together, a talent for analyzing a script and improving it by criticism and revision."

Director Lehman Engel describes his job as that of a "high priest" of theatrical production: part wizard, part business expert, part teacher. A director has to combine a playwright's

[15]

script, the skill of the actors, the expertise of stage and costume designers, the electrician's know-how, plus (for musicals) the contributions of dancers, singers, musicians, the composer, the lyricist, and the conductor. This kaleidoscope of talent and temperament must be blended into a unified, audience-satisfying experience and, if possible, a box-office triumph.

A director must understand both the make-believe characters in the play and the real actors who are going to portray them. It takes a high degree of insight and sensitivity to be successful because the "style" of a production is developed by the director. Should the play come across as nostalgic, crisply sophisticated, or tinged with sadness? Style must be carefully cultivated and everything from the scenery to the star's personality must work in harmony with that style. It can turn a play into a hit or into a flop.

A director also needs a thorough knowledge of both behind-the-scenes and front-of-the-house activities. In the professional theatre the director seldom oversees either of these areas, but in directing summer stock, regional, or university theatre, the more the director knows the better.

As a professional director you do the following when directing a play:

1. Follow the rules of Actors' Equity regarding auditions, length of rehearsals, overtime.

2. Read the play. The director *sees and hears the play being performed on a stage* as he or she reads it. It is absolutely essential that you develop this ability, and it is something you learn by yourself.

3. Make out a floor plan for every act and scene.

4. Call a first reading of the play with the entire cast.

5. Block the action. This means getting the actors moving about the stage, closely following the floor plan.

6. Set a deadline for all parts to be completely memorized.

Now the real work begins—building character, heightening conflict, creating mood—and it will continue right up to the dress rehearsals, out-of-town or preview performances, and opening night.

Even after the show opens, the director may call for an occasional "run-through" to keep the cast on its toes, to make necessary changes, or to benefit the understudies.

Training/Education

Most directors begin as actors. The reason is that few schools teach play direction as a separate course, although more offer it today than a few years ago.

You should study all phases of theatre but concentrate on acting. Get involved in as many plays as you can, if only in bit parts or in crowd scenes. You will learn to appreciate the actor's point of view, and you can observe the director at work. If you miss out on the tryouts, volunteer for the backstage crew. Then you can still attend rehearsals and take part in the production.

The job that will pay off best is that of prompter. This is more than just throwing lines to a forgetful actor. During rehearsals you hold the promptbook, you work beside the director, and whenever a comment is made about what is happening on stage, you make note of it. This is an exciting way to learn directing.

Throughout the performance you will have your hand on the pulse of the production, giving signals for entrances, sound effects, and music, thus sharpening your sense of timing and your sensitivity to audience reaction.

Opportunities

At first you may find your best chances with community or regional theatre and in summer stock. When you go to New York, your best opportunities will be on off- and off-off-Broadway. You may want to build a reputation as a specialist—directing only comedy, serious drama, the classics, or musicals. But some see specialization as a trap. They prefer to be more versatile.

Jobs leading to directing are those of actor, assistant stage manager, and stage manager. Then finally you're there at the top—as director!

DANCE

THE DANCER

A dancer is one who moves rhythmically to music, using either traditional or improvised movement and gestures. Dance can tell a story or simply delight an audience with beautiful, intricate motions. No words are necessary—only the body of the dancer is used.

To be a success as a dancer you must have talent and, in addition, an absolutely superb technique, whether you are in ballet, modern dance, or the musical theatre.

Today millions of young Americans are studying dance, but only a tiny fraction will ever make it big. Some will lose interest or discover their own lack of talent. Poor health will stop others. Dance is a vigorous art, requiring a technique second to none.

The ballet dancer's body must be beautiful in a very special way—beautiful to look at in any pose, and beautiful to watch in motion. The dancer's body must be strong and disciplined. The female dancer needs a well-proportioned body with a head set gracefully on the shoulders, and well-shaped arms and legs. Also she must have a fine instep and toes that will support "pointe" dancing. The ideal female dancer is rarely taller than five feet six inches. The male dancer, rarely over six feet, must have a fine physique and far greater strength than is apparent to the audience's eye—a controlled strength.

There are a variety of dancer types. The main ones are the ballerina and her male partner, the *danseur noble;* the supporting dancer; and the dancer of character parts.

There is also a specialized form of acting demanded by the dance. The dancer must bring to life a specific role, just as the actor does. He or she also needs a high degree of musicality, a feeling for music. But even more, the dancer must translate the accompanying musical composition into pictorial movement. Watching a skilled dancer perform, you can *see* as well as hear the composer's artistic creation.

The dancer's personality is of tremendous importance, a necessity. However, it's there within you, ready to emerge, or it's not. This is a fact that must be faced early in your training.

In American ballet, there is a dispute as to what a classical dancing company should stand for. Look, for example, at two outstanding companies, the American Ballet Theatre (ABT) and the New York City Ballet (NYCB).

The first features its stars, such as Russian defectors Mikhail Baryshnikov and Rudolf Nureyev, American ballerina Gelsey Kirkland (Baryshnikov's main partner), Fernando Bujones, and Erik Bruhn.

The sensational twenty-seven-year-old Baryshnikov insists that technique alone cannot make a great dancer. A dancer must "know what to wear emotionally in every ballet," he has said, "and how to change from step to step."

The second company, the NYCB, glorifies the choreographer and the ballets themselves, using what has been called a "treasure-trove of masterworks" by its famed directors George Balanchine and Jerome Robbins. It does not feature dancers, which does not mean that it lacks talent. It has that in abundance: Jacques d'Amboise, Suzanne Farrell, Patricia McBride, Edward Villella, to name a few.

Expressing the NYCB philosophy, Villella has said: "For us Balanchine is where the art is at. Instead of making myself the center, I look for it in the heart of the dance." In conclusion, he said: "This is our chance to work with the greatest innovator that dance has ever known—or is likely to know. Either you take it or you don't." (*Newsweek,* May, 1975.)

The "feud" between classical ballet and modern dance has faded as the two approaches have intermingled. Although modern dance still tends toward the abstract, some of Balanchine's choreography for the NYCB is just as abstract. And modern dance is once again trying to arouse the emotions of its audiences, which has always been the aim of ballet.

Training/Education
When I asked Martha Hill, director of the Juilliard School's Dance Division, what she would say to a young person who wonders whether or not to be a dancer, she replied by telling me how Martha Graham, great pioneer in modern dance, al-

ways answered the question: "No! If they have to ask that, they don't have the hard drive and the strong desire that the real dancer must possess."

If you do have the drive, then you must first look for the finest dance school in your area. Proper training is vital. To get it, turn to a school rather than an individual instructor, unless that instructor's reputation is of the highest.

A trained body is your primary goal. Training for the classical female dancer begins at about ten or eleven, before the muscles and tissues harden. Boys can begin serious study at an older age. The training for both boys and girls involves a series of exercises practiced *daily,* exercises that have been handed down from one generation of dancers to the next. They have been carefully worked out to give the dancer strength and flexibility.

Every part of your body must be disciplined in the art of the dance—your feet, ankles, legs, hands, wrists, arms, head, neck, and, hardest of all, the body frame itself. You must master a variety of steps, leaps, lifts, pirouettes, jumps, turns, and some acrobatics.

What about college? College develops the whole person. And many leading colleges and universities today have fine dance departments.

Opportunities

Ballet is enormously popular. In New York alone you can see the Royal Ballet, the Bolshoi, the Stuttgart, the NYCB, the ABT, the City Center Joffrey Ballet, and the Dance Theatre of Harlem (black classical dancers), all offering magnificent performances during the regular New York season. And most of these companies go on tour, too.

Your first break will probably be as part of the ensemble, but these performers must be just as versatile as the principal players. The more well-rounded your training, the better your chances for employment. And many a star has emerged from the ensemble.

At an audition for a Broadway show you will most likely be

asked to perform a series of classical ballet movements as they are called out to you. *Arabesque! Plié! Entrechat! Pirouette! Glissade!* If you cannot do this, stay away!

If you are one of those chosen to stay for the next test, what can you expect?

The choreographer will probably line you up in rows on stage, then perform in front of you a series of dance movements, which you will be expected to duplicate. After a while the choreographer will turn to observe your performance— and several more dancers will be eliminated. This continues until the number of dancers has been reduced to what the show script calls for plus, perhaps, two or three understudies.

In a dance career you will have one major handicap. Your "artistic" life expectancy is much shorter than that of an actor or a singer. Unless very famous, a dancer can be through at forty-five! Directors and choreographers look for younger faces and figures, dancers who can take rigorous discipline. Of course, many fine dancers become successful choreographers and directors.

That great American art form, the musical, calls for the same two basic requirements as the ballet—talent and super-technique. But you must be able to sing and act as well.

Young dancers seem more professional and more serious in pursuing their careers than other theatrical artists. They spend hours a day at the barre, doing their basic exercises, and always arrive early for auditions, rehearsals, and performances in order to limber and stretch their muscles and improve their technique. Working twelve hours a day is quite usual. In a musical a small part or walk-on will often be given to a skilled dancer over a singer, because the dancer moves more easily and correctly.

Director Lehman Engel warns that the not-really-talented, not-really-prepared may, if they have radiant personalities, get by as actors. But he adds that dancers do not. They must be *really* talented, *really* disciplined, and *really* prepared.

THE CHOREOGRAPHER

We touch on this art only briefly, because the choreographer must first understand the dance, which is covered in the previous section.

Who Is the Choreographer?
What Is Choreography?

The choreographer is the playwright of ballet and the musical and is as important to dance as the writer is to theatre. The choreographer does, in fact, write down dance notations, using signs that read like a composer's notes.

Choreography is the art of creating and arranging dances. Every top choreographer was at one time an excellent dancer. The entire ballet or dance routine you see on stage, every movement, is the creation of the choreographer, who is, in fact, the most important figure in the history of the dance.

The art of choreography developed from the days of the Renaissance dancing master, who taught nobles and their ladies the graceful movements of the pavane and the galliard.

The modern choreographer must be able to work with all the dancers in creating a ballet, must have a good music background and an appreciation of the music from different cultures, and must know acting, directing, and the pictorial theatre arts, as well as being a skilled dancer.

Training/Education

You learn the art of choreography largely through seeing others at work and by studying the creations of artists both past and present. Formal training is difficult to find, although some U.S. colleges and universities do teach choreography now. London's Royal Ballet School has made some advance in that direction, and the Juilliard School is adding this dimension to its curriculum.

You should study the history and development of dance, classical ballet, and the modern musical theatre. And study stage directing. Learn how to block stage action, how to work with performers, and how to use theatrical effects.

Opportunities

If your dream is to rise to the position of choreographer or director of a ballet company, turn back to the section of this chapter on "The Dancer." What you will have to do first will be found on those pages. Then go after the higher position. The skilled choreographer is now, more than ever, needed in the ballet, musical theatre, and opera, as well as in films and TV.

MUSIC

THE SINGER

It is a mistake for the budding singer to believe that voice is all that is needed for success. If you feel this way, change your thinking! Begin right now to plan your career as a *singing actor,* with equal emphasis on each art, and your chances for success will improve dramatically.

What Is Song?
Who Is the Singer?

A song is a musical composition, often for a single voice, a solo. Musical works for more than one voice include duets, trios, quartets, and choral ensembles. A duet, trio, or quartet normally gives the singer an opportunity to be a soloist; the ensemble does not.

Music adds something to words. Because words sung are sustained (held) longer than words spoken, the emphasis and dramatic quality are deepened.

To make the text of any song completely yours, it must be memorized. Start now to memorize poetry and worthwhile prose passages. When memorizing lyrics, give particular attention to entrances, rest periods in the music, and re-entrances.

The successful professional singer has a good to fine voice backed up with expert technique (maintained through daily vocal practice), a wide musical knowledge, and a keen intelligence. And without that last factor, all the rest can—and probably will—go right down the musical drain.

Training/Education

Proper breath control is the basis of a singer's training. It supports volume, resonance, projection, and range. The higher the tone and the longer it is held, the more breath and physical support the singer needs. Also important are tone quality (timbre) and color, which add beauty to the voice.

For the singer, as for the actor and the dancer, preparation is the keynote. This means a good education, preferably a four-year course at a school noted for its musical training. This

[28]

can lead to a Bachelor of Music, Bachelor of Science or Arts, or Bachelor of Fine Arts degree (with a music major).

At school you can absorb a lot more than voice training plus a liberal arts background. You will study the history and theory of music, the art of acting, and two additional skills—how to play the piano for self-accompaniment and how to sight-read.

Sight-reading means singing on first sight a song you have never seen before. Doing this develops a fine sense of pitch and is considered excellent ear training.

Dr. Peter Mennin, accomplished composer and president of the Juilliard School, stresses the value of the solfeggio concept, which combines vocal exercises, sight-reading, and ear training. The solfeggio method uses the "do, re, mi, fa, so, la, ti, do" of *The Sound of Music* fame.

As for the age to begin training, some feel a person should not be given voice lessons until maturity. Others believe that voice training, if wisely guided, *can* begin at an early age. But a child's voice should never be forced or strained.

As a beginner you will need strong determination and a strict sense of discipline. During your pre-college voice training you should at some point request an audition before a competent and honest voice instructor to determine if you should continue professional training at the college level.

Turn to a recognized school or conservatory of music rather than an *unknown* individual coach for training. Your music school should offer you a chance to participate in vocal workshops conducted to instill in you poise and self-confidence, or what is called "stage presence."

If you plan to teach in elementary or secondary school, you should major in music education. To teach college usually requires a master's degree or sometimes a doctorate, unless you are superbly qualified otherwise.

Personality counts because it lets you communicate with your audience, but it can be developed only if the spark is there. Take care of your appearance well ahead of time, then forget it and focus on what you are doing. Your personality will then be free to "come across."

Opportunities

As a beginner you will find the employment situation highly competitive, and the *Occupational Outlook Handbook* expects it to remain so into the mid-1980s. Opportunities do exist, however, for concert singers, church singers, recording artists, and voice instructors. Salaries vary widely. You should have a second skill to turn to in case your singing opportunities are part-time only.

If you aspire to opera, both your talent and your preparation must be first-rate. Absolutely essential is thorough training in every phase of opera—the history of opera, opera training, vocal literature, study of the famous roles, and Italian, German, English, and French diction. And you must have enough natural volume to be heard on your own without amplification.

If you are talented, disciplined, and expertly trained, you will succeed. Excellence and professionalism are essential.

When you first appear in opera or on the concert stage, you can join the American Guild of Musical Artists, Inc.

THE MUSICIAN

What Is Music?
Who Is the Musician?

You are at a performance of an American symphony orchestra. During the applause following the finale, the conductor shakes hands with one violinist, an act repeated at every symphony concert the world over.

Why? Who is the person thus singled out? It is the chief first violinist, the concertmaster, the one who leads the first-violin section, making sure that all play each passage in unison and as conducted. Though unknown to most of the audience, the concertmaster is the most important figure in the symphony orchestra. *The Wall Street Journal* (September 9, 1975) quotes conductor Arthur Fiedler as saying that the concertmaster is "the conduit through which he can transmit his ideas to the rest of the musicians," for it is the violin section that leads the entire orchestra.

Music is the "art of incorporating pleasing, expressive, or intelligible combinations of vocal or instrumental tones into a composition having definite structure and continuity" (*Webster's Third New International Dictionary*). The musician is "one skilled in music; *esp:* a composer, conductor, or professional performer of music" (also *Webster's Third*).

Unless you love music obsessively and willingly practice, practice, practice, stay away!

Dr. Peter Mennin, speaking of the strong discipline in his Juilliard music department, said that inferior students "eliminate themselves when they can no longer keep up the Juilliard pace."

Competition is stiff at this school. Only those with considerable training *before* they come to Juilliard are even permitted to audition for admission. This is true of many of the best music schools in America.

Training/Education

Technical skill comes first. As a result of many years of study, you will know and understand your instrument. Then you must be able to interpret musical compositions through that instrument. This means training and education.

Where do you get this expert training? Again, a music school or a strong college or university is preferable to an individual instructor, unless that person has a reputation for excellence and is a graduate of a reputable music school or conservatory.

There are hundreds of schools in the United States that offer four-year programs leading to bachelor's degrees in music, instrumental music, and music education. The programs cover instrument techniques and offer a wide background in the history and theory of music. Your curriculum may also include ear training, sight-reading, the literature of your instrument, the study of ensemble and chorus, improvisation, practice as soloist or with an orchestra or other music group (chamber music, string quartet), and orchestral repertoire. You will study melody and harmony, counterpoint, rhythm, instrumentation, and various music forms (fugue, sonata, opera, for example). Be certain that the school you choose is accredited by the National Association of Schools of Music.

You may find it rewarding to join with other young musicians to form your own music group, to practice together, and to perform publicly.

If you wish to teach music in elementary or secondary school, you must qualify for state certification as well. To teach in college, you will have to work toward a master's degree.

How do you know whether or not you should embark on a music career? Saul Goodman, head of the Percussion Faculty of the Juilliard School, solo timpanist, and head of the percussion section of the New York Philharmonic from 1926 to 1972, advises that you ask yourself these questions:

1. Am I doing this because I'm *vitally* interested in music?

2. Do I have the outstanding talent necessary? Am I competitive material? Can I do it better than the other person?

To answer the second question, Mr. Goodman warns that you need to be evaluated by a capable outsider—coach, teacher, or performer. The answer to both questions must be yes.

Opportunities

The principal cities of opportunity for musicians are New York, Chicago, Los Angeles, Nashville, Miami, New Orleans, and Atlanta. But you will find dance bands, vocal ensembles, and civic orchestras in many communities. Keep in mind that the *Occupational Outlook Handbook* (1974–75) expects music to remain an overcrowded profession through the 1980s. There are simply more professional instrumentalists than there are concerts and recitals to showcase them, and there is keen competition for jobs with leading orchestras. But there is *always* demand for *top* talent.

Encouraging notes are the growing number of civic orchestras (although most provide only part-time work) and the need for musicians in cable and pay TV, and for videotape cassettes.

Opportunities for the pianist are as accompanist for singers, instrumentalists, and choruses, in musicals and recitals, and in supplying mood music for, say, a restaurant. Organists play in recitals, in church, or on radio or television. The guitarist has recently gained in popularity, appearing solo or with a group. Harpists play in recital or with ensembles. All these artists frequently make recordings, classical and popular.

Musicians in major symphony orchestras that have full-year seasons may earn between $10,500 and $20,000 a year. A base salary for a beginner is about $10,500 to $12,000. Those in orchestras with shorter seasons, of course, make less and must often supplement their income by teaching or by other means. What instrumentalists in ensembles earn depends on experience, professionalism, and reputation. Teachers' earnings are determined by the school system's salary scale.

Most musical performers belong to the American Guild of Musical Artists, Inc., or the American Federation of Musicians of the United States and Canada, or both.

Cautionary note: Most performing musicians do not work steadily. So be prepared with a second skill. Music can be a beautiful, rewarding profession. But it can also be a tough one.

THE CONDUCTOR

When a symphony orchestra performs, only two of the perhaps one hundred people involved (aside from an occasional soloist) get top billing—the conductor and the composer. The same two receive the bravos at the end of the performance.

There is good reason for this. Stephen E. Rubin, in an article entitled "What Is a Maestro?" for *The New York Times Magazine* (September 29, 1974), explains why. If the conductor, as interpreter, is "sensitive enough to see through the maze of notes to what the composer was really getting at, then there occurs that incredible meeting of the minds of two geniuses that is all but unforgettable."

The conductor guides an orchestra through the interpreting of an opera or symphony composer's musical creation. This is done through the beating of meter, and by communicating with the musicians through hand signals that indicate cues for entrances, changes in rhythm and meter, the shaping of phrases, and the overall feeling of the music. Conductors have always had a strong influence on the development of musical art, especially since the eighteenth century.

Of Arturo Toscanini: "He was a fabulous conductor . . . a transformer of orchestras. . . . Toscanini would go to, say, Monte Carlo, and turn a fourth-class orchestra into a first-class orchestra . . . after only a few rehearsals. It was incredible."

—Vladimir Horowitz, pianist

"The conductor is a kind of sculptor whose element is time instead of marble; and in sculpturing it, he must have a superior sense of proportion and relationship."

—Leonard Bernstein, conductor

"I want to be someone who is considered to be a help by the players."

—Michael Tilson Thomas, conductor

Those three quotations show the transition from the old authoritarian school of conducting to the new approach of cooperation. But even when young Michael Tilson Thomas conducts, everyone knows who is in command.

Although the individual musician must be disciplined, the maestro brings together a unity of discipline necessary to establish the *modus operandi* and the ultimate performance standard that gives each orchestra its own characteristic "signature."

Training/Education

When Dr. Peter Mennin was asked what training was necessary for the aspiring conductor, he said, "The conductor must have absolute command of one instrument and a technical knowledge of all others, even if he or she can't play them. In the art of conducting, the entire orchestra is the conductor's instrument." So a conductor begins by studying music. Then he or she must develop a comprehension of the composer's art, or the structure of musical composition.

Though conducting may look easy, the conductor must actually be aware of each player, each instrument, the musical score, and the overall sound. What does the work say? What is its "architecture"? What are its principal melodies?

Superior conductors know exactly what they want and know whether or not they get it. They make their will known during rehearsals. What is a maestro's will? Simply an interpretation of the composer's purpose. And no two conductors will interpret the same composer in the same way.

Interpretation is decisive. Lorin Maazel, conductor of the Cleveland Orchestra, says that as conductor you respond so completely to those black notes that you *feel* what it is the composer had in mind. Then you win the confidence of the musicians so they will play it *your way.* Discipline *must* be maintained. Success in this depends entirely upon the force of personality and authority of the maestro.

"The conductor must also," according to musician Saul Goodman, "possess a powerful sense of rhythm and imagination within the limits of musical performance, and conform to the needs of the players and not just play to the audience."

Other requirements for success as a conductor are an accurate ear and an ability to sight-read and beat meter. The beating of meter is little understood by the uninitiated. Through it the conductor must "tell" the orchestra the beat, or impart to it the precise rhythm—accented, staccato, with a flourish, lightly, with a comic touch, poetically, loudly, or with a martial air.

Traditionally the right hand is for beating meter with a baton, and the left for indicating the musical phrase, or "chironomy." Some conductors have taken to using only their hands in beating meter. Actually, all conductors use the body, head, and eyes, as well as their hands, to convey meaning.

You can be *taught* only a portion of all this, mainly the fundamentals of musicianship. (See the section of this chapter on "The Musician.") Much of the knowledge must come by a sort of osmosis, by *watching* and then *doing.* In fact, today many schools combine learning with performing.

[35]

Opportunities

There is no question that a conductor with charisma will have no problem finding work. But either you have charisma—in this case a blend of what you are and what you have learned —or you don't.

There are many young, talented, successful conductors on the scene today, such as Daniel Barenboim, James Levine, and Michael Tilson Thomas. Some obtained assistantships with well-known orchestras. And several fine soloists have stepped from stage to podium to wield the baton. Also, the exclusive circle of the male conductor has finally been broken, by women such as Sarah Caldwell of the Opera Company of Boston and Elaine Brown of Temple University, with her "Singing City of Philadelphia" program.

A top conductor can make up to $10,000 for one performance. A tyro can expect from $750 for two concerts. The Metropolitan's highest fee for one appearance is reported to be around $4,000. Music directors' earnings differ widely, ranging from $30,000 to $150,000 yearly.

Conductors and players used to work only "in season," and the difficulties of travel often prevented them from working for more than one organization. Today concerts are given every month by several orchestras, and planes make it possible for a conductor to make many guest appearances around the world and to work for more than one organization.

THE COMPOSER

A composer creates musical composition, "the ordering of pitched sounds in musical time and space." For the composer, like the conductor, musicianship, joined to a high degree of creativity, is basic.

Frank Lloyd Wright, the famed architect, recalled his musical father's description of a symphony as "an edifice in sound." In fact, many composers, conductors, and musicians refer to musical composition in terms of structure or architecture. This conception must be understood and felt by the beginning composer.

[36]

Most composers show talent and drive very early. Composer Mana-Zucca ("I Love Life") played her first piano recital at four and was in her first large concert with the New York Philharmonic at eight. Aaron Copland *(Billy the Kid* and *Rodeo)* had chosen his career as composer by the time he was fifteen.

Women are now also achieving prominence as composers. Note the work of Pozzi Escot, Barbara Kolb, Thea Musgrave, and Shalamit Ran. And 1975 saw the Juilliard School award a doctorate in composition to a woman for the first time.

Training and education are similar to those for a musician, but special emphasis is put on writing skills and on understanding the various musical instruments. This training must come before you enroll for the specific study of composing. For someone to be accepted in musical composition at Juilliard, the catalog states that "the primary requirement is possession of a creative mind, with sufficient writing technique to make that fact apparent." Then you must submit all compositions you wrote in the last two years.

You might now try to become acquainted with the best in contemporary music, with such composers as Henry Cowell, Peter Maxwell Davies, and William Mayer. Not yet accepted by the general public, contemporary music may soon begin to build an audience. Start to listen to what the composers of our own time are saying. Note that the most lasting of contemporary music has its own definite sense of musical form and melody.

ASCAP

Some 16,300 composers and lyricists, along with 6,000 publishers, belong to the American Society of Composers, Authors and Publishers (ASCAP).

When you have copyrighted a musical work that has been commercially recorded or "regularly published," you may join ASCAP. If you have a work copyrighted but not yet published, you may apply for associate membership. (It is advisable to obtain two copyrights, one before publication and one after, in order to be fully protected.)

ASCAP protects the rights of its composer and publisher members, classical and popular, by serving as a single source of licensing and collection of royalties for those members. Another society that guards the music rights of its members is Broadcast Music, Inc. (BMI).

MUSICAL THEATRE

Versatility is the key to casting in the musical theatre. If your aim is the musical, plan a study program that will train you to move confidently from singing to acting to dancing. (This chapter deals only with the music side of musical theatre. For the two other aspects, see "The Actor" and "The Dancer.")

No matter how good your natural singing voice, don't neglect your training. Basic voice technique is as important for the popular singer as for the classical. And diction (pronunciation plus enunciation) is an essential part of this. Very few "natural" singers succeed by virtue of naturalness alone. There are exceptions, of course, like Ethel Merman, or Cyril Ritchard, who is a "speak-singer." This means the performer uses musically pitched speech to "talk" a song. It can be enormously effective.

Because of microphones, the popular singer does not need a voice of great volume, but does need the other voice qualities referred to in the section on "The Singer."

You will probably get your start in the chorus, which involves hard work, but it is stimulating, rewarding, and great experience. (Those who move from one show's chorus line to another are known as "gypsies.")

In auditioning for a show, there are several do's and don'ts for singers:

Do
☐ realize that Equity singers are heard first.
☐ look pleasant when your turn comes and concentrate on what you are doing, not on how you look. Use your anxieties to project the emotion of the lyric.
☐ know how to sight-read. This is not a necessity in musicals but it's a valuable ability in overall theatre work.

- [ ] have lead sheets of all your audition material set in your correct key.
- [ ] bring your own accompanist (perhaps your vocal coach) unless informed that a professional pianist will be on hand.
- [ ] attend every audition you can to gain ease in getting through them.

Don't
- [ ] resent it if you are not auditioned at all. There may be a good reason. You may be too tall or too short, for example.
- [ ] be surprised if you are stopped after a few bars. The director knows the type of voice needed, and yours may not be the one.
- [ ] audition a lyric until you have sung it, preferably with a coach, "at least one hundred times," says actress Violet Lane.
- [ ] audition a lyric from the show being cast, especially if it was a former hit. You will be compared with the star of that show (not to your advantage).
- [ ] hand the director a letter of introduction. It is more apt to work against you than for you.

In preparing for a career as a show pianist you need the same basic technical training as the classical performer, plus experience. You must be able to interpret all musical styles. As director Lehman Engel puts it, "Your jazz must 'swing,' your rock must 'rock.'" You must be able to play the whole score during rehearsals and to accompany soloists and chorus alike. Most show pianists are also vocal coaches. You must also be able to sight-read and transpose, to improvise (compose without preparation) upon the director's request, to remember all such experiments, and to shift quickly from one to another until a final decision is made. All this takes patience and diplomacy, in addition to musicianship.

Let me here make certain distinctions:

A *lead sheet* carries the melody, the lyric, and an indication of the basic harmony. It is set in the correct key for the individual singer by a coach, teacher, or arranger.

Sheet music purchased at a music store is set in the key chosen by the composer. Transposition to another key may be marked on the sheet above the regular bars and it is *that* that the accompanist plays.

The *score* is the music for an entire show set in the key the composer chose, with spoken cues from the show's dialogue included. Here transposition may also be written in, unless you are doing an original show with all lyrics sung in the key set by the composer.

Often there are three pianists to accompany a musical's rehearsals. Pianist 1, often a composer, works closely with the director and frequently must improvise incidental music, musical "punctuation" in certain scenes, introduction to songs (lead-ins), and musical background for dialogue (underscoring). Pianist 1 also rehearses the soloists. Pianist 2 does much the same thing for the dancers and the choreographer. Pianist 3 assists Pianist 1.

Other musicians must be prepared to play more than one instrument and in more than one style, from jazz to cha-cha, for example.

Even though it takes less immediate preparation to conduct a theatre orchestra than a symphony or opera, the basic study of music is still a must for the theatre conductor. Further, a theatre conductor needs a knowledge of stage direction, flexibility, and patience, especially in a new show when the score is completed only a short while before opening night.

The theatre conductor, besides conducting, auditions all singers, hires musicians, and works with the composer and lyricist to bring the idea of the show to life musically, and with the stage and dance directors to bring it to life visually. After the opening, the stage manager behind the scenes and the conductor out front must work together to see that each performance comes off as planned.

How do you get to the position of conductor? Begin as a musician, then become an assistant conductor (concertmaster or first violinist), and, finally, go after a job as conductor or musical director.

In musical comedy the choreographer and dance group rehearse in one studio, the musical director and singers rehearse in a second studio, and the director and principal players rehearse in a third studio. After two weeks the three groups come together and the show is "set," usually in one to two more weeks of rehearsal.

As for composer or lyricist, how do you get started? (These two may be one person, like Richard Rodgers or Jules Styne.) Again, first develop fine musicianship. Catch every live show you can, listen to radio and recordings, watch TV, read show-business papers, be attentive during classes, develop discipline to study, practice, and create effectively. Be alive to what is going on both in and out of the world of theatre. What ideas about your time need to be expressed? Can you put them to music? Can you blend the best of the past with the best of the present?

Two words of warning: (1) Don't imitate. Allow your own style to develop. If you honestly give a part of yourself, you may have a career in the making; otherwise you will go nowhere. And (2) be wary of the suggestion that if you play up to someone who has influence you will get the breaks. It won't work. There is much at stake in casting a Broadway musical —up to $1 million. So you can be absolutely certain that no director is going to hire you because you are somebody's "friend." Only talent, ability, and intelligence count. Besides, a performer is not hired by one person but by the agreement of many: for example, the stage director, the producer, and the musical director.

BEHIND
THE
SCENES

THE STAGE MANAGER

Who Is the Stage Manager?
Once a play or musical opens, the stage manager runs the show. The director becomes a spectator, watching the play from two viewpoints at the same time—gauging audience reaction, and observing mistakes by actors or crew usually obvious only from backstage.

Webster's Third New International Dictionary defines the stage manager as "one that supervises the physical aspects of a stage production." But this only hints at the thousand and one details the stage manager must oversee. Let us take a look at one production's timetable.

The stage manager first reads the play for the action and to spot those scenes that will be especially difficult to handle from a backstage point of view. The manager then attends meetings between producer and director and all auditions for casting the play. Next come discussions with the "prop" people—those in charge of furniture and smaller objects—and with the sound and lighting crew.

The scene designer gives the stage manager floor plans showing the location of exits, stage props, stairs, and windows. Then the manager chalks or tapes up the floor of the stage to give the actors the boundaries within which they must perform. Temporary chairs and tables may be put on the stage area to substitute for real stage furniture.

The stage manager guides the entire *physical* production from first reading to final performance—assigning dressing rooms, seeing that the actors are on time for the curtain by announcing over a loudspeaker, "Half hour until curtain," "Fifteen minutes," and finally, "On stage!" Then comes the signal for the curtain, and the play is under way.

Now it is up to the stage manager to see that each performance of the play goes exactly as planned, to orchestrate the work of actors, stagehands, head of props, head of wardrobe, electrician, sound technician, and musical director. And periodic rehearsals for the understudies must be organized. Yet there are no bows for the stage manager when the final

[44]

curtain falls. The audience rarely even bothers to note his or her name on the program's list of credits.

Training/Education

Aside from a knowledge of theatre production, a stage manager needs nerves of steel and must be able to maintain a delicate balance between authoritarian firmness and a fine-spun diplomacy. The manager must always uphold the age-old dictum "The show must go on." It is the manager's job to cover up mistakes so that the audience does not even suspect something has gone wrong.

A good theatre school and years of experience can prepare you for this job if you have the qualities previously mentioned.

Opportunities

No one really starts out as a stage manager. First must come years of working in theatre, both as a member of the cast and as part of the backstage crew. If you show unusual ability to handle the work and have the maturity and stage knowledge necessary, the top job may be yours eventually.

Note: As a stage manager, you must join Actors' Equity because you must interpret the union's rules for the director and the cast.

THE LIGHTING TECHNICIAN

If you plan to be a lighting expert or stage electrician, you must learn to read a script so you can isolate the practical problems as well as understand the play's purpose. You then study the entire physical theatre where the play is to be produced to determine how the required lighting can be adapted to the peculiarities of the house.

You are now ready to plan the specific lighting for each scene, taking into account the time of day in which the scene is set, the mood, the colors, sight lines, and how best to distribute the lights on stage. And you must make these ground plans to show outlets, location of spots, floodlights, border lights and striplights, and other necessary equipment.

[45]

The lighting technician must be at enough rehearsals to absorb what the director is trying to do, plan lighting effects to heighten the intended mood, and draw up the cue sheet for the dress rehearsals and performances.

The would-be stage electrician should follow the same educational road as outlined for the stage manager, with an added emphasis on lighting, and must eventually become a member of the United Scenic Artists.

THE THEATRICAL DESIGNER

No place is as lonely as an empty stage with its naked "behind-the-scenes" wall, glaring work lights, and dangling wires. Only theatre folk ever see the stage this way.

The wizard who fills this emptiness with a world created as the background for a play is the theatrical designer (scenic and costume).

Who Is the Scene Designer?

The scene designer creates stage scenery to serve as background or atmosphere for a play, ballet, or opera. The design should project a particular mood to the audience from the moment the curtain rises.

The professional scene designer needs the special ability to *see* a setting come to life while reading a script. The whole scene should take on form, perspective, color, and lighting nuances in the designer's inner vision. This is like the director's ability to see the play in action while reading the dialogue in manuscript form.

Briefly, the designer prepares sketches of ideas, gets the director's okay, and then oversees the building of the design into actual stage scenery. The designer must take into account *all* aspects of the production, including the words, music, and props.

If you are thinking about choosing this career, you must have artistic talent, a familiarity with crafts, and a love for theatre, and have worked backstage in your school drama group, in children's theatre, or for your community playhouse.

For stage design, attending college is a necessity. Consider choosing only the university or college that has its own theatre and offers a major in this difficult art.

The course offered should cover the study of scripts to determine scenic and mechanical requirements; the principles of scene painting; the construction of special properties; the drawing of floor plans and sketches; and the expansion of sketches into color renderings, elevations, and the working drawings and models to be sent to the scenic shop.

There should be a course in how to research the background of a setting to determine authenticity (Italian Renaissance, for example), a course in lighting, and an introduction to multimedia. And make sure the school also gives you practical experience in building scenery.

You might also become involved in the following: the paint shop (scenery, properties), the drapery shop (drapes, scrims, masking, upholstery), the drafting layout room where mechanical problems are worked out, the electrical shop, and (in film and television) photography, engineering, and electronics.

If you have a college degree plus at least one of your designs used in a university production, there are two ways you can get a great start. Summer stock may beckon you, offering a wealth of practical experience. Or a busy New York theatrical designer may welcome you as an apprentice.

After a successful apprenticeship you may get a chance to work on an off- or off-off-Broadway production. Designing for off-Broadway demands all your ingenuity and creativity, because three important things are in short supply there—space, money, and electrical equipment. But if your work is noted by a drama critic, it will all be worthwhile.

If in summer stock, university theatre, or off-Broadway you solve some troublesome production problems (in cooperation—never in competition—with the director), you will improve on your chances for success, and if your director moves on to better things, you may go along.

You will learn quickly that a stage design can contribute to a play's success or failure. It can enhance the director's conception of the play or negate it. A play with a delicate, romantic story, for example, can be overpowered by an overly elaborate set. And a drama with a strong theme can be weakened by a dull background.

Lighting is very important, for if a scene is lit properly, it helps to create the right atmosphere. You must understand stage lighting even if you never have to do your own. Working with the stage electrician is a vital part of the designer's job.

To be a designer of scenery, lighting, or costumes in the professional theatre, you must join the United Scenic Artists. You submit an application with a résumé of your education and experience and a list of your credits (program listings or critic's mention).

You will be interviewed by a committee and will take the union's rather stiff examination, which tests creativity, knowledge, and expertise in the various design areas.

Who Is the Costume Designer?

A vital part of any theatrical production, the costume designer has to work out how the performers should look and move. The actor who plays Charlemagne (eighth century) and the actress who plays Marie Antoinette (eighteenth century) must not only look like those characters but must *move* as Charlemagne and Marie Antoinette moved in their different historical periods.

Costume designs should be "an extension of the set," writes John Gassner in *Producing the Play.* As a designer you need to know a play's historical and geographical setting and any specific problems affecting the costumes. For example, in designing for Shakespeare's *The Taming of the Shrew,* you must keep in mind that some of Katharina's costumes get pretty rough handling.

Following your own research, you must present to the director sketches of costumes that will blend with the scene designer's setting. Your finished costumes must also enhance the actors' characterizations. And aside from looking right, the clothes must feel comfortable so the actors can easily perform all the action required by the script. To accomplish this you need a thorough understanding of fabrics, color, line, accessories, and the effect of light on both costume and makeup.

Educational requirements are varied. You will need creativity, an ability to draw and sew, and a knowledge of history, dramatic literature, art, and the details of theatrical production.

Obtain catalogs from several colleges and examine them carefully. Are there courses to cover the areas listed above? Is the theatre department known for its excellent productions? Is the student given an opportunity to design actual costumes for a play? When all answers are yes, you have found your school.

SELECTED LIST OF THEATRE SCHOOLS

The following lists do not include the many fine college and university theatre departments throughout the country, with one or two exceptions and for the reasons given. You should investigate yourself the possibilities within your own city and state. Most schools and studios listed herein specialize in one or more of the performing arts.

California
Actors Studio, Los Angeles
Actors Theatre Workshop, Los Angeles
California State University, Northridge (Summer Teen-age Drama Workshop)
Pasadena Playhouse
Professional Theatre Workshop, Hollywood

The Lee Strasberg Theatre Institute, Hollywood
Three Arts Studio, Santa Monica
Video Tape Workshop, Los Angeles

Colorado
Hacker Theatre School, Denver
Little Theatre of the Rockies, Univer-

sity of Northern Colorado, Greeley
(scholarship program granting tuition; summer)

Connecticut
Eugene O'Neill Memorial Theatre
Center, Waterford (encourages
young playwrights; summer)
White Barn Theatre, Westport
(summer)

Florida
Guild Players Foundation,
Jacksonville
Studio M Playhouse, Coral Gables

Illinois
Goodman Memorial Theatre, Chicago
Theatre Art School, Oaklawn

Maine
Three Arts Studio, Portland

Massachusetts
Leland Powers School, Boston
Stage One Theatre Laboratory,
Boston
Williston-Northampton School,
Easthampton

Minnesota
The Guthrie Theater, Minneapolis

New Hampshire
Hampton Playhouse, Hampton

New York
Stella Adler Theatre Studio, New York
City
American Academy of Dramatic Arts,
New York City
American Musical and Dramatic
Academy, New York City
Chautauqua Summer School
Circle in the Square Theatre School,
New York City
Clark Center for Performing Arts, New
York City
Department of Cinema Studies, New
York University, New York City
(emphasis on cinema)

Dramatis Personae, New York City
H. B. Studio, New York City
Helen "Teddy" Hall, New York City
High School of Performing Arts, New
York City
Institute for Advanced Studies in the
Theatre Arts, New York City
The Juilliard School, Lincoln Center,
New York City
Robert Lewis Theatre Workshop,
Irvington-on-Hudson
Sonia Moore Studio of the Theatre,
New York City
Neighborhood Playhouse School, New
York City
New York Academy of Theatrical
Arts, New York City
Riverside Theatre Workshop, New
York City
Roundabout Theatre Company, New
York City
Showcase Theatre Dramatic School,
New York City
Lee Strasberg Theatre Institute, New
York City
Television Studio School of New York,
New York City
Weist-Barron TV School, New York
City

Ohio
Cincinnati Academy of Theatre
Cleveland Play House
Willson-Frazier School, Columbus

Pennsylvania
Hedgerow Theatre School, Moylan
Philadelphia Drama Workshop,
Philadelphia

Texas
Alley Theatre, Houston
Dallas Theatre Center

Washington
Cornish School of Allied Arts, Seattle
Directors Studio, Seattle

Wisconsin
Wisconsin Conservatory, Milwaukee

SCHOOLS OF DANCE

California
Academy of Ballet, San Francisco
Ruth St. Denis, West Hollywood
School of the San Francisco Ballet

Connecticut
Theatre Component, American Dance
Festival, Connecticut College, New
London

District of Columbia
National Ballet School, Washington
Washington School of the Ballet

Florida
Imperial Studio, Palm Beach

Illinois
Allegro American Ballet School,
Chicago
Western Illinois Summer Music
Theatre, Macomb (accepts
apprentices)

Iowa
University Theatre, University of Iowa,
Iowa City (musicals and opera;
accepts apprentices)

Maine
Brunswick Music Theatre, Bowdoin
College, Brunswick (accepts
apprentices)

Maryland

Broadstreet Musical Stage and School, Silver Spring (summer)

Massachusetts

The Boston School of Ballet

Jacob's Pillow, Lee

National Center of Afro-American Artists, Roxbury (drama, music, and dance)

North Shore Music Theatre, Beverly (accepts apprentices; classes—summer)

South Shore Music Circus, Cohasset (same as North Shore)

New Jersey

Newark Ballet Academy

New York

Alvin Ailey American Dance Center, New York City

American Ballet Theatre School, New York City

American Musical and Dramatic Academy, New York City

Ballet Arts, New York City

Merce Cunningham Studio, New York City

Dance Notation Bureau, New York City

The Martha Graham School of Contemporary Dance, New York City

Harkness House of Ballet Arts, New York City

Robert Joffrey Ballet School, New York City

The Juilliard School, New York City

Charles Lowe School of Dancing, New York City

Melody Fair, N. Tonawanda (summer)

Metropolitan Opera Ballet School, Lincoln Center, New York City

National Academy of Ballet, New York City

New Dance Group Studio, New York City

School of American Ballet, New York City

Charles Weidman School of Modern Dance, New York City

Igor Youskevitch School of Ballet, New York City

Ohio

Ballet Russe School, Cleveland

Pennsylvania

Civic Light Opera Association, Pittsburgh (accepts apprentices)

Mansfield Festival Theatre, Mansfield (musicals; apprentices may earn college credit)

Philadelphia Civic Ballet

Pittsburgh Playhouse School of the Theatre

Texas

Houston Ballet Foundation

Utah

University of Utah Department of Dance, Salt Lake City (offers a degree in dance)

Washington

Cornish School of Allied Arts, Seattle

For a list of literary agents write:
The Society of Authors' Representatives, Inc.
101 Park Avenue
New York, N.Y. 10017
For a list of local residences for performing arts students, write the school of your choice.

SCHOOLS OF MUSIC

Connecticut
Yale University School of Music, New Haven

Maryland
Peabody Conservatory of Music, Baltimore

Massachusetts
New England Conservatory of Music, Boston

New Jersey
Westminster Choir College, Princeton

New York
Eastman School of Music, University of Rochester

Juilliard School of Music, New York City

Manhattan School of Music, New York City

The Mannes College of Music, New York City

Turtle Bay Music School, New York City

Ohio
Oberlin College Conservatory of Music

Pennsylvania
Curtis Institute of Music, Philadelphia (scholarship only)

PUBLICA- TIONS CARRYING THEATRE NEWS

Backstage
165 West Forty-sixth Street, New
 York, N.Y. 10036
$18 per year

Billboard
1 Astor Plaza, New York, N.Y. 10036
$50 per year

Ross Reports
150 Fifth Avenue, New York, N.Y.
 10011
$12 per year

Show Business
136 West Forty-fourth Street, New
 York, N.Y. 10036
$15 per year, $8.00 for six months

Summer Theatres
(a special annual)
136 West Forty-fourth Street, New
 York, N.Y. 10036
$3.50 a copy

Theatrical Calendar
171 West Fifty-seventh Street, New
 York, N.Y. 10019

Variety
154 West Forty-sixth Street, New
 York, N.Y. 10036
$30 per year

[55]

FOR FURTHER READING

Barthel, Joan. "The Master of the Method Plays a Role Himself." *The New York Times,* February 2, 1975.

Bentley, Eric. *The Theatre of Commitment and Other Essays.* New York: Atheneum, 1967.

Burton, Philip. *Early Doors: My Life and the Theatre.* New York: Dial Press, 1969.

Clurman, Harold. *The Divine Pastime: Theatre Essays.* New York: Macmillan, 1974.

Dalrymple, Jean. *Careers and Opportunities in the Theatre.* New York: E. P. Dutton, 1969.

Engel, Lehman. *Getting Started in the Theater.* New York: Collier Books, 1973 (paperback).

Fergusson, Francis. *The Idea of a Theater.* Garden City, N.Y.: Doubleday, 1949.

Funke, Lewis, and Booth, John E., eds. *Actors Talk About Acting.* New York: Avon Books, 1973 (paperback).

Gambling, John. *Rambling With Gambling.* Englewood Cliffs, N.J.: Prentice-Hall, 1972.

Gassner, John. *Directions in Modern Theatre and Drama.* New York: Holt, Rinehart, 1966.

———. *Masters of the Drama.* 3rd ed. New York: Dover, 1953.

———. *Producing the Play,* bound with the *New Scene Technician's Handbook* (Philip Barber) rev. ed. New York: Holt, Rinehart, 1953.

Gorelik, Mordecai. *New Theatres for Old.* New York: E. P. Dutton, 1962 (paperback).

Guthrie, Tyrone. *My Life in the Theatre.* New York: McGraw-Hill, 1959.

Hartnoll, Phyllis. *The Concise History of Theatre.* New York: Harry N. Abrams, no date (paperback).

Kerr, Walter. *Tragedy and Comedy.* New York: Simon & Schuster, 1967.

Kirstein, Lincoln. *Dance: A Short History of Classic Theatrical Dancing.* New York: G. P. Putnam, 1935.

Köhler, Carl, and Von Sichart, Emma. *A History of Costume.* New York: Dover, 1963 (paperback).

Mayer, William. "Live Composers, Dead Audiences." *The New York Times Magazine,* February 2, 1975.

The New Encyclopaedia Britannica (in 30 volumes—The Macropaedia). Chicago: Encyclopaedia Britannica, 1975. (This all-new version of the famous encyclopaedia has excellent and comprehensive articles on all phases of the performing arts.)

Rockefeller Panel on the Performing Arts. *The Performing Arts: Problems and Prospects—a Report.* New York: McGraw-Hill, 1965 (and paperback).

Rowell, Kenneth. *Stage Design.* New York: Reinhold, 1968 (paperback).

Rubin, Stephen E. "What Is a Maestro?" *The New York Times Magazine,* September 29, 1974.

Stanislavski, Constantin. *An Actor Prepares.* New York: Theatre Arts, 1936.

Stuart, Donald C. *The Development of Dramatic Art.* New York: Dover, 1960 (paperback).

Taper, Bernard. "Balanchine Is a Prism That Refracts Music Into Dance." *The New York Times,* November 17, 1974.

Warre, Michael. *Designing and Making Stage Scenery.* New York: Reinhold, 1966.

White, Edwin, and Battye, Marguerite. *Acting and Stage Movement.* New York: Arco, 1963 (paperback).

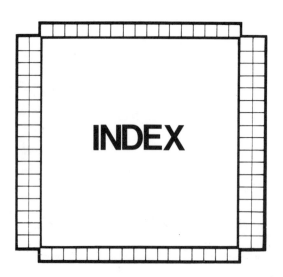

INDEX

ABOUT THE AUTHOR

After graduating from Marygrove College in Detroit, Louise Horton earned her M.A. as a speech major at the University of Michigan. She has been a director for university, community, and children's theatre groups in several states, and has taught at the College of Saint Catherine in St. Paul, Minnesota; the University of Denver; and Mercy College, in Detroit.

Miss Horton, now a resident of New York City, works for the American Society of Interior Designers. She has authored for Franklin Watts another in our Career Concise Guide series, *Art Careers*.